Interesting Facts about Homer's Odyssey

Greek Mythology Books for Kids
Children's Greek & Roman Books

BABY PROFESSOR

EDUCATION KIDS

Speedy Publishing LLC

40 E. Main St. #1156

Newark, DE 19711

www.speedypublishing.com

Copyright 2017

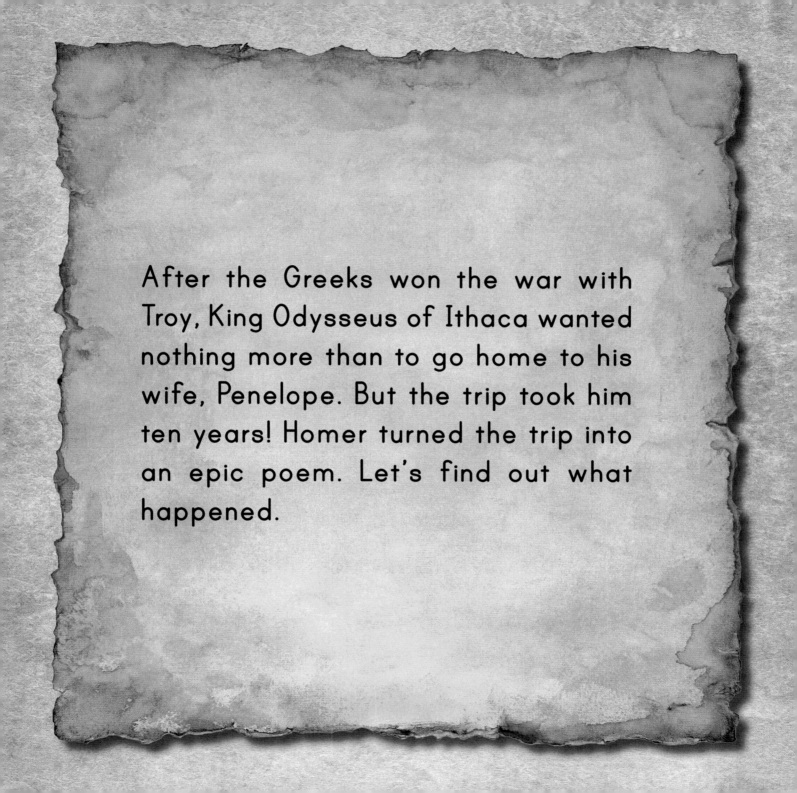

After the Greeks won the war with Troy, King Odysseus of Ithaca wanted nothing more than to go home to his wife, Penelope. But the trip took him ten years! Homer turned the trip into an epic poem. Let's find out what happened.

WHAT'S AN EPIC POEM?

Gilgamesh, written in Sumeria, and Homer's Iliad and Odyssey, are three examples of epic poems. Epic poems usually look like adventure stories when you read them quickly, but they deal with serious questions about heroism, national character, and what human life is all about. There is far more in them than just fighting the bad guys or escaping from the monsters, although there is plenty of that, too.

Tablet of Gilgamesh

Homer and his guide

WHO CREATED THE ODYSSEY?

Homer, a blind poet active in Greek Ionia in the 8th century BC, put together the Iliad and its sequel, the Odyssey.

Homer may have been born in what is now Turkey, and he may have lived on the island of Chios, whose people used to call themselves Homeridae.

Chios Island

Statue of Homer

The events Homer told about took place about 400 years before he was born. He used traditional stories, legends everybody knew, and traditions about the war with Troy, as well as adding his own plot lines, events and descriptions.

Homer put together these epics for performance, like a poetry reading, and he probably went from city to city in Greece sharing his remarkable story. People learned the poems by heart and they weren't written down for a very long time.

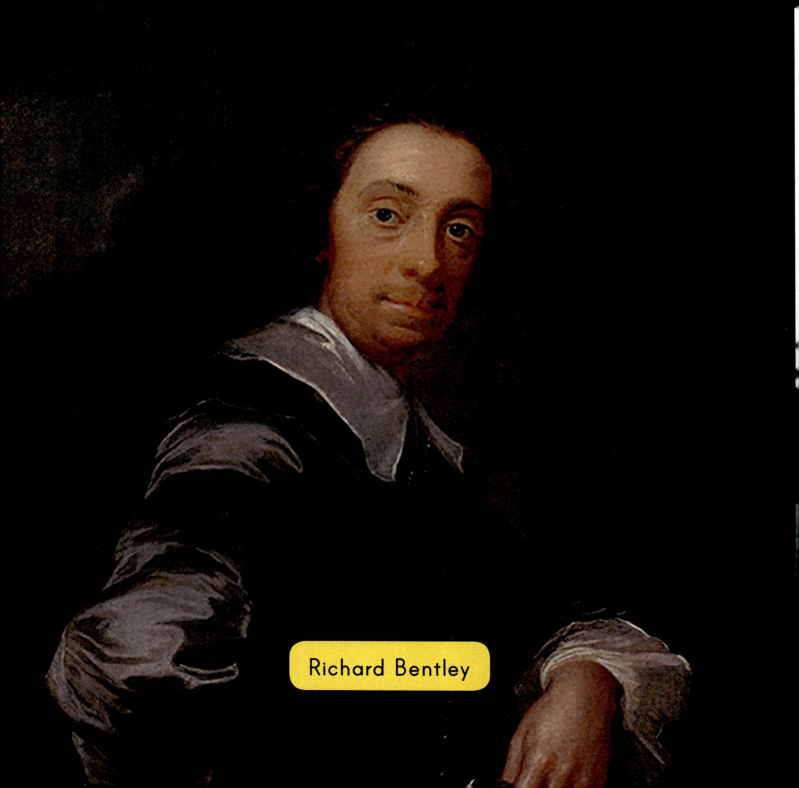

Richard Bentley

Some people think that parts of the poems were written by other people. Richard Bentley, an English critic, wrote that much of the Odyssey was probably written by one or more women. He argues that the women's characters are complex and interesting, while the male characters are typical adventure heroes.

He also points out that in the Odyssey there are a lot of details, like correctly folding laundry, that women would have cared about more than men. Some of the details about ships, which men presumably would have known more about (though not necessarily a blind poet!), seem incorrect.

HOMER (NINTH CENTURY B

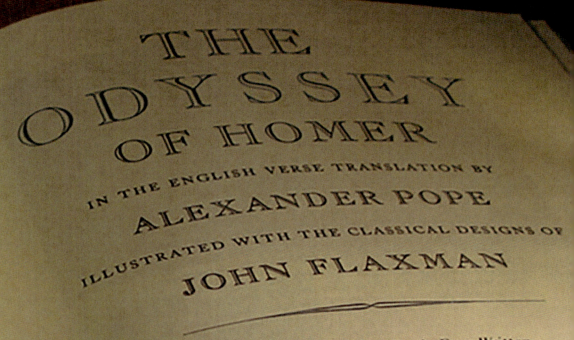

THE ODYSSEY
OF HOMER

IN THE ENGLISH VERSE TRANSLATION BY

ALEXANDER POPE

ILLUSTRATED WITH THE CLASSICAL DESIGNS OF

JOHN FLAXMAN

The 100 Greatest Books Ever Written

Collector's Edition
Bound in Genuine Leather

The Easton
NORWALK, CON

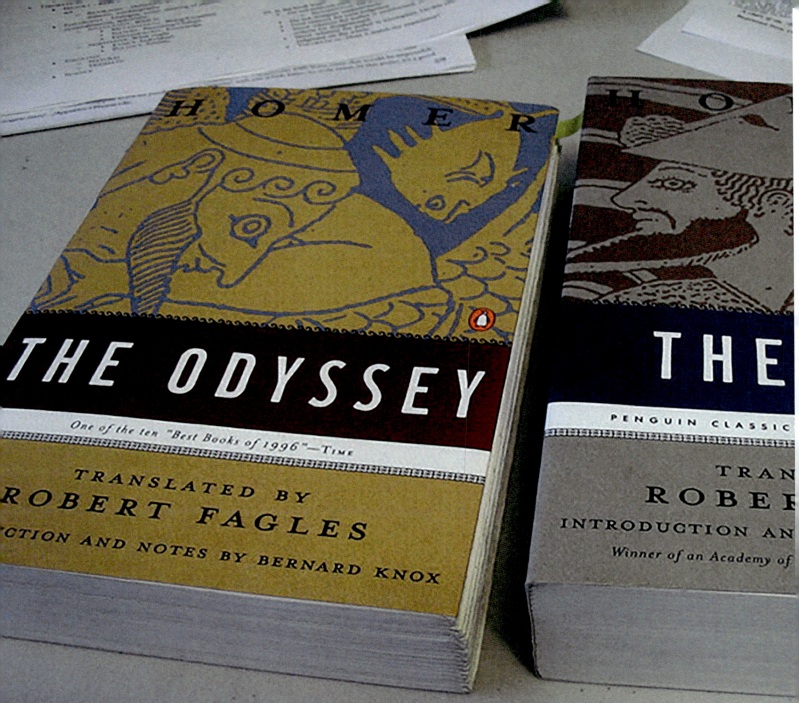

HOMER

THE ODYSSEY

One of the ten "Best Books of 1996"—Time

TRANSLATED BY
ROBERT FAGLES
...CTION AND NOTES BY BERNARD KNOX

HO...

THE...

PENGUIN CLASSIC...

TRAN...
ROBE...
INTRODUCTION AN...
Winner of an Academy of...

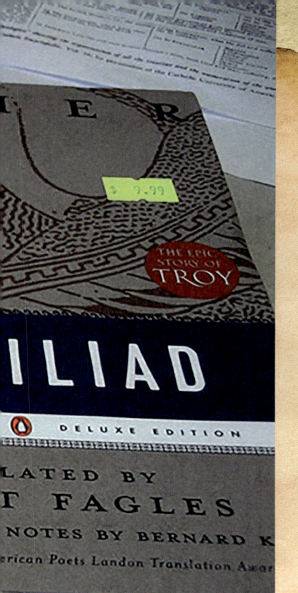

Other critics have pointed out that the two poems use many different Greek dialects and words specific to local areas. It is as if, in a novel claiming to be written by someone in New York, one chapter sounds like it was written in Texas and the next chapter is full of slang common in Jamaica.

THE SHAPE OF THE STORY

In the Iliad, the armies of Greece go off to war with the great city of Troy, in what is now Turkey. There are many reasons for the war, but the main one is that Paris, a prince of Troy, captured the heart of Helen, wife of King Menelaus.

Trojan War

Helen of Troy

Helen was reputed to be the most beautiful woman in the world. Paris took her away to Troy with him, and the armies of Greece followed to bring her back.

The war took ten years. At the end, Troy was defeated and Helen returned to her husband. Many Greek heroes fought and died against Trojan heroes, and the gods pitched in to help or hinder both sides.

In the Odyssey, at the end of the Trojan War, Odysseus and his men set sail for home. The journey should only take about three weeks, but it lasts ten years. Monsters, storms, the will of the gods, and a range of distractions slow Odysseus down.

THE STRUCTURE OF THE POEM

The Odyssey has 24 books, divided into an opening and three sections. In performance, the poet probably recited a single book at a time, leaving the audience anxious to hear more, both the parts they already knew and the parts the poet was creating.

Poseidon

The opening

As the poem opens, Odysseus has been gone from home for almost 20 years, and is frustratingly close to completing his journey. He is an unwilling guest on the island of Calypso, a sea goddess, who wants to keep him as her lover. The sea god, Poseidon, is angry at Odysseus and will not let him cross the ocean between Calypso's island and his home.

THE FIRST SECTION: IN ITHACA

At home in Ithaca, after 20 years without news of Odysseus and almost ten years since the rest of the Greek army returned to their homes, everyone thinks Odysseus must be dead. Rich and powerful men position themselves to marry Penelope, who must be a widow, and take over the kingdom. Odysseus' son, Telemachus, worries about how to protect his mother and wonders if the men will kill him if he gets in their way. Penelope tries various tricks to avoid making a decision about whom she will marry. She is faithful to Odysseus and is sure he is still alive...but it has been twenty years.

Ithaca

The second section: The long journey

In the second section, Odysseus tells the story of everything that happened to him and his men since they left Troy in twelve ships. Some of the highlights:

THE LOTUS EATERS

At the island of the Lotus Eaters, some of the crew eat plants that make them want to give up their trip home and stay on the island. Odysseus can barely get his men away.

Island of the Cyclops

The Island of the Cyclops

The Cyclops Polyphemus captures Odysseus and some of his men in a cave. The one-eyed monster eats six of the crew before Odysseus can blind him. Then the men can escape. Unfortunately, Polyphemus is a son of Poseidon, the sea god, who makes things difficult for the rest of the voyage.

The Winds of Aeolus

Aeolus, the god of the winds, gives Odysseus a bag of winds to use to get his fleet home. But his men open the bag at the wrong time, and the winds blow them far away from Ithaca.

Laestrygonians

The Laestrygonians

The Laestrygonians are giant women who throw boulders at Odysseus' ships, sinking all but one ship and killing most of his men.

The Island of Circe

Circe lures the crew onto her island and turns them into pigs. Odysseus has to use all his cunning to rescue them.

Circe

Sirens

THE SIRENS

The ship has to pass the land of the Sirens, who sing so enticingly that they draw men close, and eat the men after their ships are wrecked on the rocks. Odysseus has his crew block their ears with bees' wax so they cannot hear the song. He has himself tied to the mast because he wants to hear, and is almost driven mad with desire to go to the island.

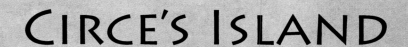

CIRCE'S ISLAND

After many more adventures, all of the crew are lost and only Odysseus makes it as far as Circe's island. She lived alone, and is happy to force Odysseus to be her companion for seven years. At the end of that time, with the aid of the gods, Odysseus is able to leave the island, cross the sea, and reach Ithaca.

Odysseus

The Final Section: The Return

Home again, but isolated among many potential enemies, Odysseus disguises himself as a beggar until he can learn what is going on in his palace. His loyal dog recognizes him. He meets with his son Telemachus, and together they plan what to do.

Penelope has run out of ways to delay making a choice for her new husband. She says she will pick the one who can string Odysseus' great bow and shoot a quiver of arrows with it, and can then throw an axe through the holes in a row of other axes (the shape of the axe blade and the shaft left a gap through which, by a miraculous throw, another axe might be able to pass).

Penelope

None of the suitors can even string Odysseus' bow, much less use it to shoot arrows. Odysseus asks if he can try, and the suitors mock him, thinking he is a mere beggar. Odysseus takes the bow and strings it easily. Then he throws the axe through the other axes. While the suitors are still reacting, he uses the bow and arrows to kill them. The floor of the great hall is littered with bodies and drenched in blood. In that grisly scene Odysseus reunites with Penelope and their fortunes are restored.

Homer's Influence

People say that the Iliad and the Odyssey are part of the basis of European culture. They not only set the form of how to tell a story; they provided guidance for moral living, what makes good or bad men and women, and how society should function.

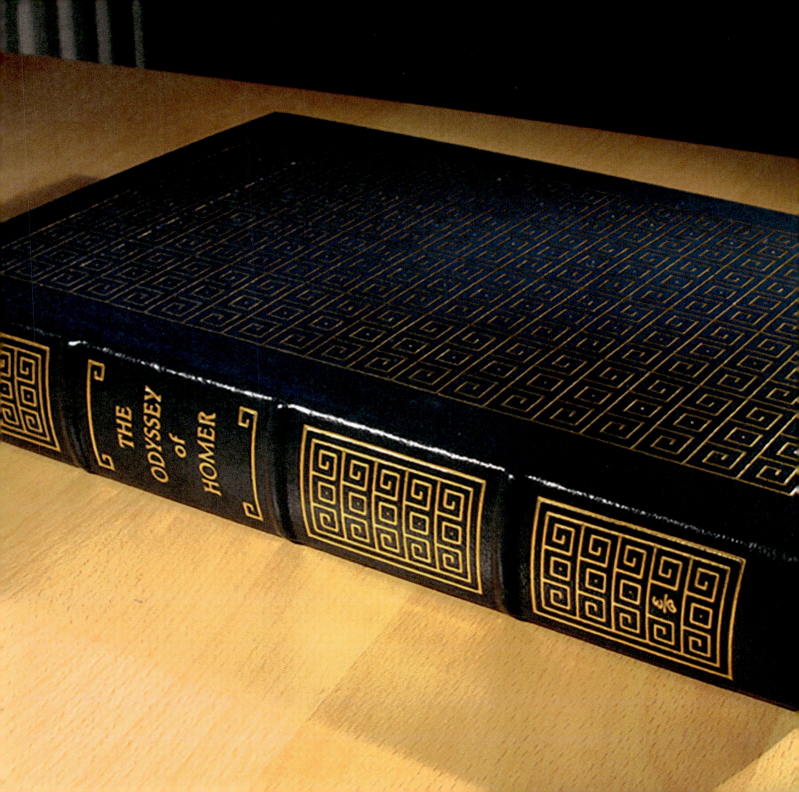

Aeschylus

For Greeks and Romans, they were sources for history, moral conduct and religious rituals. The great Greek playwright Aeschylus said, "Everything I write is but little slices from the great feast that Homer prepared."

Epics, myths and legends

Stories from all around the world inspire us with tales of great heroes, dangerous monsters and wonderful events. Other Baby Professor books can help you learn about Norse gods, King Arthur and his knights, and the heroes and villains of many other stories.

Visit

BABY PROFESSOR
EDUCATION KIDS

www.BabyProfessorBooks.com

to download Free Baby Professor eBooks
and view our catalog of new and exciting
Children's Books

Made in the USA
Coppell, TX
04 August 2021